CONQUERING YOUR FEARS

THE CORNERSTONE PUBLISHING

Debbie A. Ajayi

Conquering Your Fears
Living A Life Without Limits!

Copyright © 2020 by **Debbie A. Ajayi**

Paperback ISBN: 978-1-952098-00-0

Printed in the United States of America. All rights reserved solely by the publisher. This book or parts thereof may not be reproduced in any form, stored in a retrieval system, or transmitted in any form by any means - electronic, mechanical, photocopy. Unless otherwise noted, Bible quotations are taken from the Holy Bible, New King James Version. Copyright 1982 by Thomas Nelson, Inc., publishers. Used by permission.

Published by:
Cornerstone Publishing
A Division of Cornerstone Creativity Group LLC
Info@thecornerstonepublishers.com
www.thecornerstonepublishers.com
516.547.4999

Author's Contact
For booking to speak at your next event or to order bulk copies of this book please use information below:
+1 (516) 205-0972
deborah.oni@gmail.com

CONTENTS

Acknowledgments..7

Introduction..9

1. The Enemy Within..11

2. Anatomy of Fear..21

3. Why You Must Prevail Over Fear....................39

4. The Other Side of Fear...................................55

5. Rouse the Champion in You..........................69

6. Failure is Not the End....................................81

7. Divine Assurances in Fearful Times................93

ACKNOWLEDGMENTS

First and foremost, I'd like to give thanks to God Almighty, because without Him none of my accomplishments amount to anything.

I deeply appreciate my wonderful husband, Timothy Ajayi, for his constant love and encouragement throughout this project. I thank my lovely children, Danielle and Gabrielle, for their understanding and support as mommy inevitably spent much-needed hours away from playtime!

I am forever indebted to my lovely parents, Titus and Victoria Oni, for their unceasing encouragement and support, and also my awesome sisters and their spouses, Esther and Michael Falodun, Drs. Dayo and Ruth Abdulkareem, and Elizabeth and Yomi Adisa, who have always been immensely supportive of my goals and ambitions through the years.

A special thank you to Ruth, who used her expert skills during the initial editing of this book and generously provided necessary technical suggestions during this project.

My heartfelt gratitude goes out to these amazing group of family members, friends and colleagues, who in many ways, graciously provided inspiration, goodwill and moral support: The Folarin Family, Anita Porter, Taiwo and Bisi Oladapo, Stephen Akintayo, Seyi Hopewell, Mbet Umanah, Lydia and Oreoluwa Fawole of Lydore Music Network, Ria Millen, Angela Braddox, Seyi Alabi, Kristel Noezil, Seun Obaloju, Xannee Dreckett-Richards, Dr. Tosin Apara, Funmilayo Atandare, Olutayo Ajayi, Penny Moukas and Morenike Omotosho.

You all have been awesome. God bless you richly!

INTRODUCTION

Fear is one of our most primeval emotions. It is a natural reaction to our awareness of the numerous dangers that lurk around us and our inherent limitations as mortals to effortlessly foresee and forestall these hazards.

But then, instinctive or imaginary awareness aside, most of the realities that daily rattle our world, especially in present times, are undeniably frightening. Even the most courageous of men will readily affirm that the times in which we live are particularly peculiar - or to use scriptural language, perilous. What with the ravages of strange diseases and natural disasters, the frequent and frenzied assault on faith, morality and decency, the increasing ingenuity of evil minds in unleashing terror on their fellow men, the seeming helplessness of governments to safeguard the lives of citizens or guarantee availability of basic needs, and of course, the perpetual shrinking of economic resources in sharp contrast to the exploding number of people desperately jostling for these scare resources.

What this means is that both within and without, we are besieged by the sights, sounds and even smells of fear. This naturally makes us prone to allowing fear to dominate our minds and regulate our lives. Yet, being prone to fear is not the same as being powerless before it. In other words, the fact that we are surrounded by fear does not mean we must be subdue by it. We can rise above fear, master it and even make it work for us. Strategies for achieving this are what you will be reading throughout the pages of this book.

Whatever your fears are, you are about to be empowered - mentally, psychologically, physically and spiritually – to confront and triumph over them. A bolder, stronger and greater you is about to emerge. See you on the other side of fear!

1

THE ENEMY WITHIN

"It's not our enemies that defeat us, it is our fear."

— **Anon**

Walking through the streets of Kowloon in Hong Kong, one day, Norman Vincent Peale sighted something that surprised him so much that he had to stop to get some explanation. According to his own narration, it was a tattoo studio he had sighted and in the window were displayed samples of the tattoos available. The artist had placed different pictures that any customer could ink on their body. However, what caught the passerby's attention among the display samples was an inscription containing three words: BORN TO LOSE.

As a foremost motivational speaker and writer, Norman was shocked beyond words and had to enter the shop to confront the Chinese tattoo artist. Pointing at the inscription, he asked the man, "Does anyone really have that terrible phrase, 'Born to lose', tattooed on his body?" To which the man replied, "Yes, sometimes." "But," Norman stuttered, "I just can't believe that anyone in his right mind would do that." The Chinese man simply tapped his forehead and said in broken English, "Before tattoo on body, tattoo on mind."

It was then Norman got the message: it all begins in the mind. It was not about the tattoo artist or the inscription on display – those were just external forces helping to manifest what had already been settled on the inside of the customer. And I am telling you this because we all are so prone to doing what Norman did. We spend so much time and energy blaming the wrong factors and fighting the wrong forces as being the cause of the limitations that we experience in our lives. We wish things were different on the outside – that we would have fewer challenges, more opportunities, greater support, better resources and wider connections. Yet, we ignore the fact that none of these "limiting forces" can actually hold us down for long without the active involvement of our greatest enemy, our own fears.

I don't know the "tattoo artist" that you currently have in your life. The one you consider to be the reason you are not living your best life. The one you usually blame for not being able to maximize your potentials, follow

The Enemy Within

your passion or fulfill your dreams. I often hear some of these perceived enemies from the people I interact with. Disability. Troubled upbringing. Unsupportive family. Financial difficulty. Stifling environment. Limited opportunities. The list goes on. But, whatever yours is, you may be surprised to discover that your real enemy is not any of these. If you think deeply about it, as I'm sure you will in the course of reading this book, you may discover that the actual enemy holding you down and from which you must detach yourself, is the fear prowling right within you.

Trust me, I am not in any way attempting to belittle the gravity of your situation or the severity of what you have to deal with. I understand how daunting and frustrating some circumstances can be – whether it's within your family or your school or workplace. But, friend, the truth is that the solution or breakthrough you need is not the sudden collapse of these seeming barriers; the solution could be in you finding the courage to demolish the stronghold of fear that these challenges have progressively built within and around you.

Indeed, from the moment you find your courage, your perspective about your life and circumstances automatically changes. You will suddenly discover that most of what you consider to be barriers are actually ladders and what you consider to be stumbling blocks are actually stepping-stones. In fact, it may surprise

Conquering Your Fears

you that the same place that you have always seen as a confinement, or even worse, a graveyard of destiny, could suddenly become a goldmine from which you will achieve what you would never have thought possible. And most importantly, you will realize that you are stronger, smarter and greater than you've always thought you were.

PRACTICAL SCENARIOS

Let me show you a practical demonstration of how this enemy within exerts its dominion over our lives, while giving us the impression that our challenges come from the forces around us. Imagine waking up in the morning and dreading to go to your job, all because of the range of unpalatable experiences you may have to endure from your colleagues, clients or superiors. It may seem as if those colleagues and bosses are your problem; but really, it is the fear that you have developed about your encounters with them that is making life difficult for you. The moment you decide to subdue this fear by critically assessing your situation and devising strategies for survival and success, you will find yourself in control again as the storms around react to your new-found courage and gradually subside.

Or perhaps you are a student and you have developed a fear of going to school because you do not believe you have what it takes to make it through the day.

The Enemy Within

You are particularly worried about the challenging learning materials that will be presented, which you are absolutely sure you will not understand. Consequently, this fear controls you to the point of making you fail your coursework, get reprimanded by your parents, or get into trouble with the school authorities. Again, while it may seem reasonable or convenient to blame the learning materials and other factors within the school for what you are going through, the truth is that your challenge stems from the fact that you have allowed your fears about these factors to prevent you from addressing them appropriately.

I can relate to these experiences because these were some of the fears I personally had to confront to make progress and succeed in life. I will reveal more details about this shortly, but before then, let me point this out: there is nothing you cannot accomplish if you set your mind to it. If I was able to conquer my fears in different areas of my life, I want to let you know that you can do the same. Do not give up! You must work on having a positive mindset and an "I-can- do" mentality. This will empower you to persevere and build your confidence, a vital asset in achieving your goals.

CHALLENGING TIMES

In my younger years, I was what people would refer to as an average student. And this was primarily because I almost always entertained the fear of not making it top in my class. I did not have a mentor to push or convince me to believe that I was intelligent and smart enough to pass all my exams or succeed in life. With this fear of failure came a very low self-esteem, as I did not believe in myself. This affected my grades through middle and high school.

Upon graduating from high school, I enrolled in a two-year college program. I chose a two-year program because I didn't think I could study and excel for four straight years. To me, that was torture! So, I entertained the thought that once I finished my two-year program, I would proceed to learn a trade and call it a sweet day. That was it. That was my master plan!

While in college, I was determined to give it my best shot so that I could pass all my classes. With this determination came many challenges, especially from my fellow students, several of whom were quite intimidating and downright mean. However, I remained resolute in my commitment to succeed.

Thankfully, at the end of that two-year period, I passed all my courses with flying colors. It was at that point that the feeling and experience of success made me to consider the possibility of furthering my education. I transferred my credits and enrolled in a four-year university program. To my complete surprise, I graduated with a bachelor's degree in two years and was on the Dean's List for both years of study!

The Enemy Within

I must say, however, that graduating from college did not come on a platter of gold. I faced several challenges, some of which threatened to oust me from school. One of those challenges was the fact that I had to get a job while in school. Combining schoolwork with a part-time job was tough for me. Nonetheless, I knew I had to do it, if I was to have some financial stability in school. I remained determined to push through and succeed. This resolution led me to enroll in an after-school tutoring program that helped me to achieve success with several challenging courses.

After I graduated, my next challenge was to get a well-paying job to take care of student loans, bills, and everything else in-between. I began my search for employment by sending out job applications to many organizations of interest. For a while, it was difficult to gain employment in my field of study, and for the most part, I was turned down due to limited work experience.

After a few months of sending out job applications and getting rejected, I finally secured a job and was over the moon about it. Little did I know that another challenge was lurking just around the corner. I resumed work at my new office, and no matter how hard (or smart) I worked, it became increasingly apparent to me that I would have to, figuratively, pass through the eye of the needle, to get promoted or move up the corporate ladder.

Conquering Your Fears

The unfortunate phenomenon of gender discrimination was rearing its ugly head right in my workplace. The harder women worked trying to advance their careers, climb up the corporate ladder and break barriers, the more resistance they appeared to encounter! This realization led me to the decision to pursue a higher degree. This, to me, would equip me with specialized skills and competencies and provide a better chance of securing employment where my worth was valued and appreciated.

Once again, I was scared. I wondered if I could excel at this higher-level education program because I now had a full- time job to combine with it. I sought the counsel of some of my mentors and was encouraged to enroll in a two-year part-time master's degree program.

Turning Fear into Fortune

During my very intensive program, I was able to stay focused and, within a year and a half, graduated with distinction! I achieved this with sheer determination and perseverance. I remember the many long nights of sleep deprivation, trying to complete assignments, prepare for projects and examinations. There were also long, tiring drives home from school, during which I sometimes found myself drifting in and out of sleep. I am very grateful to God for keeping me safe through it all.

The Enemy Within

Upon graduation, I approached the human resources (HR) department at one of my previous places of employment and informed them about my intention to pursue a position of interest. Although I knew that I did not have the stipulated years of work experience needed to occupy that position, I remained optimistic as I was now armed with an advanced degree.

It so happened that a few months later, the position of interest became available, and the HR department approached me with an offer to fill that position. I was also informed that, although training would be offered for the first few weeks, I would need to work hard to catch up with the work demands. It seemed quite challenging at first, especially having to interact and work with colleagues with various perspectives and personalities. It was a fast- paced work environment that motivated me to adapt quickly to my new role.

It has indeed taken me gradual but deliberate steps to achieve the personal and workplace success I have today.

I owe many thanks to God and to the team I worked with, who believed in me and encouraged me to succeed. Additionally, the different experiences I had gone through while I was in school came in very handy, as I was able to apply lessons learned to overcome the challenges I was confronted with at work.

Conquering Your Fears

YES, YOU CAN

I shared these personal experiences to encourage you that it is possible to conquer every mountain and attain your goals and dreams – once you have first conquered the enemy within. Your external battles become much less daunting once you've learned to subdue this internal contender with your destiny. As Robert Greene rightly says, "Your fears are a kind of prison that confines you within a limited range of action. The less you fear, the more power you will have and the more fully you will live."

The point here is that, you, my friend, can achieve success despite your challenges and fears. Convert your fears to forces of inspiration to keep you going, rather than letting them imprison you in self-doubt and self-sabotage. Yes, you can. Regardless of what people or circumstances tell you, you can be anything and do anything you set your mind to!

2

ANATOMY OF FEAR

"Of all the liars in the world, sometimes the worst are our own fears."

— **Rudyard Kipling**

With all that we have explored in the first chapter, especially from the personal experiences I shared, one thing should have become very clear to you: Fear is both as powerful and powerless as you desire it to be. This may sound contradictory, but it is nonetheless true. When you allow fear in your life, it quickly expands itself, takes over every fiber of your being, paralyzes your potentials, blinds you to opportunities and possibilities, and instigates you to take actions according to its dictates alone. And as you can be sure, actions dictated by fear are often devoid of reason and, sometimes, decency.

On the other hand, if you decide to take charge of your life, despite the whispers and pressures of fear, then you suddenly and surprisingly realize that fear is just a phantom, an illusion that only takes whatever shape you make of it. This is why many have come to define fear as False Evidence Appearing Real. Napoleon Hill puts it even more succinctly, "Fears are nothing more than a state of mind."

Well, since our main mission here is mastering the strategies and principles for conquering our fears, we must go further to demystify fear and fully understand the nature and workings of this enemy within. This is important because it is in knowing the truth that we will realize how much damage we are allowing fear to do to our potentials and progress in life. And with this truth, we will be better positioned for deliverance from its power and influence. I pray for you that before the end of this book, every chain of fear would have been broken in your life.

FEAR UNMASKED

So, what exactly is fear? It has been well-described as "an unpleasant, often strong emotion, caused by anticipation or awareness of danger." Another source describes it as "a distressing emotion aroused by feelings of impending danger, evil, pain, etc., whether the threat is real or imagined."

Anatomy of Fear

Three very important facts are contained in these descriptions. The first is that fear is one of the many emotions that we possess as humans and express from day to day. The second is that it is triggered by feelings and expectations of danger. The third and most important fact, however, is that these perceived dangers are not always real. They are, more often than not, only conjured and fired up by our own imaginations.

Now, it is important to explain why fear has become an integral part of our emotions because being a part of our emotions could easily be interpreted to mean that we were created to be vulnerable to fear. This further gives the impression that fear could be from God Himself. But nothing can be farther from the truth. The Scripture clearly says that "God has not given us the spirit of fear, but of boldness, love and a sound mind" (2 Timothy 1:7). And we know that God's word is absolutely true. This brings us back to our original question. What is the origin of fear?

Fear is one of the repercussions of our fall in the Garden. There is no fear in heaven or in the presence of God because God is love and there is no fear in love. Besides, perfect love casts out fear (1 John 4:8,18). What the angels and the children of God manifest to God is holy reverence – not slavish fear. This means that fear, just as other negative emotions like guilt, shame, jealousy, anger and hate, was never God's intention for us. Why would we need to fear when all that God made was good?

But then came Satan with his wiles to cause mankind's fall, and with that came the first-ever mention of the negative emotion of fear in the nature of man. Genesis 3:9-10 says, "Then the Lord God called to Adam and said to him, "Where are you?" So he said, "I heard Your voice in the garden, and I was afraid because I was naked; and I hid myself."

Get it clearly then, friend, that fear was never in God's original blueprint for you or for mankind in general. It's one of the earliest pointers to man in his fallen, defeated and confounded state. What this implies therefore is that fear is not for conquerors and champions; it is for the vulnerable and the vanquished. I'm sure you don't want to be categorized among such groups of people. This is why you must begin to wage war against fear in your life.

The Biological Dimension

Perhaps you have begun to wonder: Is it then possible to live life entirely without fear? Is it possible never to be afraid of anything, not even obvious danger or threat throughout one's lifetime? My answer to that is no. And, here, I must make an important clarification. You see, fear manifests in either of two distinct forms.

Anatomy of Fear

There is the normal fear, which is basic and instinctive, and which is possessed by every human. There is, on the other hand, the abnormal fear, which is the fear we are waging war against here and which you must never allow in your life.

What do I mean by normal fear? As I already pointed out, mankind ceded our dominion over the earth to Satan and his demons when we fell in the Garden. This invasion by these evil forces has made the once safe and peaceful earth to become a habitation of dangers and cruelties (Psalm 74:20). Several evils that couldn't have been imagined before the fall of man – accidents, death, attacks, sicknesses, diseases, deprivations and so on – have become possible realities. And, of course, with these realities has come the emotion of fear, which began with Adam and has been passed on to every one of its descendants afterwards.

I believe that God has particularly allowed this fear instinct to be passed on to the generality of humanity and to remain with us because we need the instinct to survive and thrive in the deformed and dangerous condition that the earth has assumed following the giving up of our authority to the evil one. Revelation 12:12 says, "Therefore rejoice, O heavens, and you who dwell in them! Woe to the inhabitants of the earth and the sea! For the devil has come down to you, having great wrath, because he knows that he has a short time."

Let me put it simply – the normal fear instinct has been left with us to combat the various actual physical dangers we may encounter throughout our sojourn on earth.

This fear instinct is meant to trigger in us what is known as the "fight or flight" response when faced with an actual physical danger - say for instance, a raging fire, a collapsing bridge, a charging bull or a rampaging shooter. This "fight or flight" response comprises a spontaneous chain of reactions in our body and mental faculty that helps us to deal with the danger. Once this fear sets in following the perception of a potential danger, our body releases hormones that slow or shut down functions not needed for immediate survival (such as our digestive system), while heightening those functions that might help us survive (such as our eyesight). In addition, our heart rate and respiration increase, blood flows to our muscles and they become tense, while our mind becomes more alert, all preparing us to either run from the danger or stand and fight.

This means that without this basic fear instinct, not only would we just rush headlong into dangers but we would also be physically and psychologically powerless to deal with them. Providing more insight on this, an expert wrote: "When we sense danger, the brain reacts instantly, sending signals that activate the nervous system. This causes physical responses, such as a faster

Anatomy of Fear

heartbeat, rapid breathing, and an increase in blood pressure. Blood pumps to muscle groups to prepare the body for physical action (such as running or fighting). Skin sweats to keep the body cool. Some people might notice sensations in the stomach, head, chest, legs, or hands. These physical sensations of fear can be mild or strong."

Abnormal Fear

Basically, therefore, normal fear is a survival instinct in us that warns us of danger and prepares to escape it. Things however become abnormal when this emotion, with all the associated biological and psychological reactions that are meant to be automatically triggered at a time of immediate physical danger become a permanent or frequently occurring feature of a person's life and begins to interfere with their peace and progress.

You can also easily tell that fear has assumed an abnormal dimension when it is triggered in anticipation of an imagined threat, as opposed to actual threat. This happens, for instance, when someone wants to write an exam, make a presentation, meet someone new or undertake some other tasks and begins to panic in expectation of failure, defeat, criticism or humiliation.

We will be looking fully into the damaging powers of fear in the next chapter. But I'm sure you can very quickly deduce one of such with the biological changes in the body (caused by fear) occurring when they are actually not needed. Lots of things go wrong when there is an abuse. Consequently, when chemicals in the body that are meant to be occasionally secreted to deal with immediate dangers are frequently triggered for non-existing and imagined threats; or when bodily functions are frequently altered to deal with perceived dangers without eventually achieving any significant purpose, you can easily guess what the short and long-term consequences will be.

As Celestine Chua, writing about why we should overcome fear, has rightly noted, "Having increased blood flow to muscles, restricted blood flow to stomach and dilated pupils do not help us in those scenarios. If anything, we might make worse moves due to these biological reactions. Imagine someone rambling off on the stage due to his or her stage fright. Or someone making a wrong career decision as he or she could not process the information clearly."

SHADES OF ABNORMAL FEAR

A dimension of this permanent sensitivity to fear as I mentioned above is what is commonly known as phobia. Phobia is a persistent fear of a situation, activity, or thing that causes the victim to want to avoid it. This fear manifests with a deep sense of panic every time

Anatomy of Fear

the source comes to your mind or you encounter it. Experts have identified the three major types of phobias as social phobia (fear of public speaking, meeting new people, or other social situations), agoraphobia (fear of being outside), and specific phobias (fear of particular items or situations).

Another dimension of this abnormal manifestation of fear is paranoia. This involves having extreme feelings of distrust and suspicion about others and believing that they are very likely to harm you. More specifically, paranoid people constantly suspect the motives of those around them, with the feeling that people in general, are "out to get them." Paranoid people naturally have problems getting along with others and they do all sorts of outrageous things to "protect" themselves from the attacks or hurts that they frequently expect to come from those they relate with.

According to Mental Health America, some identifiable beliefs and behaviors of individuals with symptoms of paranoia include mistrust, hypervigilance, difficulty with forgiveness, defensive attitude in response to imagined criticism, preoccupation with hidden motives, fear of being deceived or taken advantage of, inability to relax, or argumentativeness.

Yet another aspect of abnormal fear, which comes from mere imagination or expectation of something bad happening, is what is known as anxiety. Anxiety is a feeling of apprehension about what is to come. It is a strong feeling that is driven by the forces of negativity and makes one to expect that an anticipated event will likely go wrong or that some unpleasant happenings may occur in the near or distant future. With anxiety (or excessive worrying), the mind and body go into overdrive as one constantly focuses on "what might happen."

It is exactly this dimension of fear that Christ warns against in Matthew 6:25-27, saying: "Therefore I say to you, do not worry about your life, what you will eat or what you will drink; nor about your body, what you will put on. Is not life more than food and the body more than clothing? Look at the birds of the air, for they neither sow nor reap nor gather into barns; yet your heavenly Father feeds them. Are you not of more value than they? Which of you by worrying can add one cubit to his stature?"

These are manifestations of fear that God Almighty by His infinite power wants to uproot from your life. You really shouldn't be bound by phobias, paranoia or anxiety at any time in your life. You are the redeemed of the Lord, the child of the King of kings and Lord of lords!

Anatomy of Fear

SCRIPTURAL DIMENSION

While behavioral scientists and psychologists can offer us some explanations on the different ramifications of fear, it is the Scripture that provides us with the most authoritative, insightful and liberating truths about what this emotion entails. As you explore these perspectives, you will understand better how God expects you to see fear and why you must forcefully reject it in your life.

1. Fear is a spirit

Yes, my friend, things get much more serious from here. What we are dealing with is not just some biological feeling but a spirit. In the same way that Satan and his demons can easily infiltrate the emotions of anger (turning it to destructive rage) and love (turning it to lust), there is also a spirit behind abnormal fear, the purpose of which is to subject you to a lifetime of limitations, torment and misery.

It is for this reason that the Scripture says, "For God has not given us a spirit of fear, but of power and of love and of a sound mind" (2 Timothy 1:7). This scripture makes it clear that whenever you observe any fear that you know is not an instinctive reaction to immediate physical danger, then you should know that there is a spirit at work, with a destructive assignment to accomplish. And it is for you to resist it, so that the enemy will have no say in your life.

What makes the spirit of fear more dangerous is that it easily opens the door of our lives for other destructive forces to invade. As a result, once fear takes root in an individual's life, several other ills begin to manifest. I once read an article in the Virginian Pilot, which stated, "One of the first and foremost door openers to other demonic spirits is the spirit of fear. This spirit can take on many forms, but its intentions are clear, no matter what kind of spirit of fear it may be. It intends to keep you from fulfilling the destiny that God has on your life; from living a joyful, spirit-led existence where you give to others out of the overflow of love in your life."

In other words, once the seed of fear is allowed to take root, several other dangers follow. This apparently explains why God repeatedly warns His people to reject and resist fear in all its manifestations (see, for instance, Deuteronomy 3:22, Joshua 1:9 and Isaiah 43:1).

2. Fear involves torment

1 John 4:18 says, "There is no fear in love; but perfect love casts out fear, because fear involves torment." You realize that you are dealing with abnormal or satanic fear, when whatever it is you are thinking about subjects you to prolonged emotional torture and anguish. You may even find yourself having repeated nightmares, panic attacks and hallucinations.

Anatomy of Fear

Perhaps the most common manifestation of fear as torment is in the pains that usually accompanies anxiety. The torment comes from the fact that the anticipated evil is expected to happen in the near or distant future. This means that throughout the duration of the time the "evil" is being awaited, the biological and psychological reactions that accompany fear must occur in the life of the individual again and again. This is where the torment comes from.

Explaining why abnormal fear and torment go hand in hand, Jim Elliff, president of Christian Communicators Worldwide, says, "Future worry is overwhelming. There's a reason. We don't have grace today for tomorrow. One of Satan's simplest tricks and most effective devices is to draw our attention to things we can do nothing about. There's nothing worse than a crisis that can't be fixed. If our hours are spent with thoughts of tomorrow's problems, which are not accessible today and which we know we cannot touch with today's resources, we are doomed to worry. And worry wears us out…"

The tormenting power of fear also comes from the frustration of being unable to make meaningful decisions, despite knowing the right thing to do. It is indeed tormenting to know that you could probably do something quite well, yet do not want to try because of fear. Equally tormenting is the haunting belief that the world is against you or that you are the next person to fall ill or die prematurely.

Interestingly, as analyses have shown, 40 percent of an average person's fear is focused on things that will never happen, 30 percent on things about the past that can't be changed, 12 percent on things about criticism by others, mostly untrue, 10 percent on health, which gets worse with stress and 8 per cent on real problems that will be faced. But even with the 8 per cent, much of the power and will to combat the problems if they eventually emerge would have been drained by the torment suffered by the anxious mind. As Ian Maclaren says, "What does your anxiety do? It does not empty tomorrow of its sorrow, but it does empty today of its strength. It does not make you escape the evil; it makes you unfit to cope with it when it comes."

3. Fear is a bondage that must be broken

The Scripture in Hebrews 2:15 describes some people "who through fear of death were all their lifetime subject to bondage." This reveals clearly that abnormal fear functions like a bondage, a bondage that can last a lifetime, if conscious steps are not taken to break it. Bondage has been described as slavery or involuntary servitude. Abnormal fear therefore is one that makes you do things against your wish. Also, just like it happens in slavery, abnormal fear is one that places you in social, spiritual, mental, emotional or professional confinement, such that you cannot fully fulfill your potential.

Fear becomes a bondage when it places a sort of embargo on your life that regulates your activities. A state where you find yourself being terrified of nearly everything and everyone. When you find it so difficult expressing yourself, even when there's a lot for you to say, because you believe everyone is out to criticize and condemn you; when you keep hearing negative voices in your head, shutting you down whenever you want to take vital steps and initiatives towards recognition and progress in life; when leaving your home daily becomes a source of concern or when you dread making certain moves or taking certain decisions because of past hurts or failures - then you must realize that the bondage of fear is at work.

This bondage of fear is what breeds the different kinds of phobias that exist in people's lives. I even discovered that this bondage can assume such outrageous dimensions in some people that they become scared of discarding some things in the trash, even though that's where such things rightly belong! This phenomenon is described as hoarding. An author explains that for these folks, "getting rid of their stuff (even trash) is tantamount to removing a limb." What bondage!

Channels of Fear

Most times, abnormal fears do not simply develop on their own. The enemy often exploits certain encounters, experiences and circumstances to sow the seed. When these seeds are detected and neutralized, using the strategies we shall be considering in a later chapter, the power of fear is prevented from taking hold of the individual's life. However, if any of these seeds is nurtured through the response of fear that the enemy expects, then the seed steadily grows and takes over a person's entire being and life. Such channels through which the enemy sows the seed of fear include:

1. **Previous traumatic experiences.** This could be physical, sexual or emotional abuse, harsh criticisms, negative comments; failures, attacks, accidents, disappointments and so forth. With such negative occurrences, the seed of fear is sown, such that the individual expects the cycle to continue or that the negative remarks may be true, after all.

2. **Unpleasant experiences of others.** Sometimes we assume that since others have failed, then we too must fail. We assume that since others, perhaps in our family line, suffered a certain fate, then it must happen to us too.

3. **Negative reports and diagnosis.** Dreadful reports, analyses and forecasts by supposed experts are

exploited by the enemy to make us apprehensive. Quite often, too, negative medical diagnoses and reports are effective channels of fear.

4. **Prevailing unpleasant circumstances.** Issues such as general economic downturn, raging natural disasters, fast-spreading epidemics or catastrophic weather conditions can cause unnecessary panic, if care isn't taken. Even as children of God, we sometimes erroneously believe that since accidents, infections, terrorist attacks, job loss, business collapse and other misfortunes are happening all around, then it should happen to us too.

5. **Analysis paralysis.** When we are prone to excessive risk analysis before taking an action, we may find ourselves becoming so fearful that we are unable to take any meaningful step towards the path of progress. Constantly overthinking even small decisions can trigger worry and anxiety at any point in time.

Of course, there are many other channels through which the seed of fear is sown in us. Whether yours is among those listed or not, what matters most now is that your time to break off the hold of fear over your life has come. It is a decision you have to make because the consequences of allowing fear to fester in your life are more horrible than you can ever imagine. Let's examine some of these potential perils.

3

WHY YOU MUST PREVAIL OVER FEAR

"Fear is an insidious and deadly thing. It can warp judgment, freeze reflexes, breed mistakes. Worse, it's contagious."

— **Jimmy Stewart**

An ancient story has it that, one day, a man driving a carriage to Constantinople was stopped by an old woman who asked him for a ride. He took her up beside him and, as they drove along, he looked at her and became frightened. So, he asked, "Who are you?"

"I am Cholera," the old woman replied. Now, even more alarmed, the man ordered the old woman to get down and walk; but she persuaded him to take her along, promising that she would not kill more than five people in Constantinople. As a pledge of the promise, she handed him a dagger, saying to him that it was the only weapon with which she could be killed. Then she added: "I shall meet you in two days. If I break my promise, you may stab me."

Shortly after, news broke out that over 120 people had died of the cholera in Constantinople. The enraged man who had driven the old woman to the city, and to whom she had given the dagger as a pledge that she would not kill more than five, went out to look for her. When he eventually found Cholera, he raised his dagger to kill her. But she stopped him, saying: "I have kept my agreement. I killed only five. Fear killed the others."

This illustration might be just a parable, but it is a true reflection of what happens in real life. Indeed, it has been proven, historically and scientifically, that fear kills and destroys more people more than most of the diseases and misfortunes we may think of. Many of the tragedies that we witness daily and many of the medical conditions that send people to their untimely graves are either triggered or worsened by fear. As a thinker has observed, "Where disease kills its thousands, fear kills its tens of thousands. The greatest miseries of mankind come from the dread of trouble rather than from the presence of trouble. From the cradle to the grave fear casts its baleful shadow. Fear betrays man's spirit, breaks down his defense, disarms him in the battle, unfits him for the work of life, and adds terror to the dying bed."

Why You Must Prevail Over Fear

What I want you to understand here is that fear usually comes into our lives to accomplish a destructive mission. Therefore, you must refuse to allow its germination or incubation in your life. Once, when asked to give advice to young golfers, Sam Snead who was widely regarded as one of the greatest golf players of all time, said, "Of all the hazards, fear is the worst". Explaining what this means, another professional player said, "Fear, lack of confidence and that negative voice inside your head can ruin a good round." This is as true in life as on the field of play. Here then is a list of reasons you must reject fear in your life:

1. Fear wastes destiny.

I'm sorry, if that sounds a bit harsh, but I really cannot think of a more powerful force on earth that has hijacked and sabotaged the destinies of multitudes of people more than fear. Many people that should have been celebrated achievers and people of impact on earth have ended their lives in penury and obscurity, simply because they were too afraid to develop their talents, follow their passion or take the necessary steps that could have helped to birth their greatness. They simply were too afraid to act on the ideas, initiatives and talents that God had given them because of fear of failure, criticism or rejection. Unfortunately, many of them went to their graves unknown and unsung.

Capturing this tragic consequence of fear, the late Myles Munroe is quoted as saying: "The wealthiest place on earth is not the oil fields of Iraq, Iran, Saudi Arabia or Kuwait. It is not the diamond mines of South Africa, Zimbabwe or the Democratic Republic of Congo. The wealthiest place on earth is the cemetery, the graveyard. You may wonder, why is the graveyard so wealthy? It is because in the cemetery are books that were never written, paintings that no wall will ever see. The graveyard is filled with music that no one has ever heard and poetry that no one will ever read, ideas that will never be reality. The cemetery is filled with great men that died as alcoholics and drug addicts; it is filled with powerful women that died as prostitutes; it is filled with dreams that will never come to pass; it is filled with businesses that will never open. What a tragedy!"

I pray for you that your destiny will not be wasted.

2. Fear paralyzes ability and sinks initiatives.

It is rather unfortunate that most of the people who fail at certain tasks and in certain situations such as during examinations or interview, do not do so because they lack ability but because they allow their fear to get the better part of them. Once fear sets in, even the most intelligent and talented person appears powerless and unsuitable. The reason is because fear messes with our brain's processing ability and memory functions, such that we are unable to understand or recall lots of information that we would have been able to handle ordinarily.

Fear has equally sunk many great initiatives that had started well and could have become record-breakers. This usually happens when after starting something awesome, you start hearing voices in your head or from people around you that what you're trying to do is unthinkable or impossible. Here is a classic example from the Scripture on how this works:

"Now in the fourth watch of the night Jesus went to them, walking on the sea. And when the disciples saw Him walking on the sea, they were troubled, saying, "It is a ghost!" And they cried out in fear. But immediately Jesus spoke to them, saying, "Be of good cheer! It is I; do not be afraid." And Peter answered Him and said, "Lord, if it is You, command me to come to You on the water." So He said, "Come." And when Peter had come down out of the boat, he walked on the water to go to Jesus. But when he saw that the wind was boisterous, he was afraid; and beginning to sink he cried out, saying, "Lord, save me!" And immediately Jesus stretched out His hand and caught him, and said to him, "O you of little faith, why did you doubt?" (Matthew 14:25-31).

You see, Peter had already started doing what he was divinely commanded and empowered to do, but he made the mistake of paying attention to the negative vibes from his environment. What followed immediately was that he began to sink. This is what fear has done and continues to do to the potentials of many.

3. Fear breeds vulnerability.

Fear doesn't make the feared object or situation become less fearsome; rather it makes the victim more powerless to confront it. In an article reviewed by mental health practitioner, Sue Towey, it is stated that "fear can impair formation of long-term memories and cause damage to certain parts of the brain, such as the hippocampus. This can make it even more difficult to regulate fear and can leave a person anxious most of the time. To someone in chronic fear, the world looks scary and their memories confirm that."

But even worse is that, as we have earlier seen, fear opens the windows and doors of a person's life for invasion by all sorts of destructive forces. First fear makes one to be vulnerable physically. Experts have found that fear weakens our immune system and can cause cardiovascular damage, gastrointestinal problems such as ulcers and irritable bowel syndrome, as well as decreased fertility. It can also lead to accelerated ageing and even premature death.

Second, fear leads to spiritual vulnerability. It is a normal strategy in warfare not to present oneself as being vulnerable to the enemy. Once Satan knows that he has succeeded in planting the seed of fear in someone, he begins a cycle of torment in the individual's life by penetrating their defenses and showing them more reasons to be afraid. Worse still, he could use the advantage of this weakened defenses to attack any area of the person's life.

Consider the case of Elijah, who despite being a mighty prophet, allowed fear to gain access in his life through the threats of Jezebel. Immediately, the seed of fear penetrated his heart, the fire of depression and hopelessness was released upon him and he began talking of death and other unpleasant things. 1 Kings 19:1-4 narrates, "And Ahab told Jezebel all that Elijah had done, also how he had executed all the prophets with the sword. Then Jezebel sent a messenger to Elijah, saying, "So let the gods do to me, and more also, if I do not make your life as the life of one of them by tomorrow about this time." And when he saw that, he arose and ran for his life, and went to Beersheba, which belongs to Judah, and left his servant there. But he himself went a day's journey into the wilderness, and came and sat down under a broom tree. And he prayed that he might die, and said, "It is enough! Now, Lord, take my life, for I am no better than my fathers!"

Third, fear makes us vulnerable in our relationships. Fear often breeds feelings of insecurity and low self-esteem, which often leads to clinginess in a relationship. And, when, by our clingy nature, we give people the impression that we don't consider ourselves to be anything without them in our lives, it makes it easy for us to be exploited and maltreated.

I have known employees who continue to get abusive treatments from their employers from year to year, simply because they make it appear like they cannot survive without working in such organizations. And of course, I have seen people who get repeatedly abused by their partners simply because they gave the impression that their worth was dependent on retaining such abusive partners in their lives.

4. Fear leads to wrong decisions.

Since fear hampers our brain functions and is often driven by negative forces, it goes without saying that one of its hallmarks is to lead you into taking wrong decisions, shortcuts and quick fixes – the damaging consequences of which can be permanent. A mental health specialist explains that fear can interrupt processes in our brains that allow us to regulate emotions, read non-verbal cues and other information presented to us, reflect before acting, and act ethically. This impacts our thinking and decision-making in negative ways, leaving us susceptible to intense emotions and impulsive reactions. All of these effects can leave us unable to act appropriately. I noted in the previous chapter that actions dictated by fear are often devoid of reason and sometimes of decency. The Scripture is particularly replete with practical examples of people who took such actions and the terrible consequences that followed. Sarah, in Genesis 16, was consumed by the fear that she and her husband might die childless – despite the promises God had made to them. She therefore pressured Abraham into having a child by her maid. At first, the plan seemed to work, but soon after, both Sarah and Abraham realized that they had committed a serious blunder. The maid became very disrespectful to Sarah and Sarah transferred the aggression to Abraham and their once peaceful home was thrown into crisis. The saddest part is that, even though they tried to remedy the situation by sending the maid and her child away, the damage caused by that impulsive decision which was taken out of fear continues to haunt and convulse the entire world to date.

The two daughters of Lot too allowed the fear of remaining unmarried to push them into committing abominations. Here is what happened: "Then Lot went up out of Zoar and dwelt in the mountains, and his two daughters were with him; for he was afraid to dwell in Zoar. And he and his two daughters dwelt in a cave.

Now the firstborn said to the younger, "Our father is old, and there is no man on the earth to come in to us as is the custom of all the earth. Come, let us make our father drink wine, and we will lie with him, that we may preserve the lineage of our father." So they made their father drink wine that night. And the firstborn went in and lay with her father, and he did not know when she lay down or when she arose. It happened on the next day that the firstborn said to the younger, "Indeed I lay with my father last night; let us make him drink wine tonight also, and you go in and lie with him, that we may preserve the lineage of our father." Then they made their father drink wine that night also. And the younger arose and lay with him, and he did not know when she lay down or when she arose. Thus both the daughters of Lot were with child by their father" (Genesis 19:30-36).

You see the way fear impairs reasoning here? First, the daughters erroneously assumed that there was no man on earth to have a relationship with them. Yet, God's word clearly says that He who made them at the beginning made them male and female (Genesis 5:2) – which implies that there is always someone for everyone. Secondly, the daughters didn't mind manipulating their father and dishonoring their own bodies (as many still do today), just to have their way. It was an impulsive decision but the consequences were severe, as both of them gave birth to children who were not only accursed, but their descendants also proved to be perpetual thorns in the flesh of the people of God, the Israelites.

Naomi and her family too allowed fear to breed desperation in them. There was a temporary period of famine in the land that God had placed them, but they allowed desperation to push them into leaving the place of blessing into an accursed land. Well, even though they seemed to get the food they were hankering after, it wasn't long before the dreadful consequences of their decision began to manifest. Naomi lost her husband and her two children in quick succession and she was forced to return to the land of Israel, a much poorer person. The lamentation she gave at her return was particularly touching, "But she said to them, "Do not call me Naomi; call me Mara, for the Almighty has dealt very bitterly with me. I went out full, and the Lord has brought me home again empty. Why do you call me Naomi, since the Lord has testified against me, and the Almighty has afflicted me?" (Ruth 1:20-21).

This example of Naomi reminds me of a story I read about recently. It was stated that not long after September 11, a woman from the Boston area who had flown dozens of times announced to her family several states away that she was now afraid to fly and would instead drive to a family function the next weekend. Sadly, however, she was killed in an automobile crash on the way. Fear of a statistically lower risk (flying) led her to engage in a behavior that has a much higher risk (driving), and that fear cost her life.

5. Fear drains time and energy.

Edmund Burke says, "No power so effectually robs the mind of all its powers of acting and reasoning as fear." What does one gain from worry and anxiety? Nothing. As Jesus asked, "which of you by worrying can add a cubit to his stature?" (Matthew 6:27). We only waste precious time and energy that could have been put into profitable use and developing coping strategies when we spend time worrying.

William James says, "If you believe that feeling bad or worrying long enough will change a past or future event, then you are residing on another planet with a different reality system." And Mary Hemingway adds, "Worry a little bit every day and in a lifetime you will lose a couple of years. If something is wrong, fix it if you can. But train yourself not to worry. Worry never fixes anything."

6. Fear cripples growth.

The reason many individuals enjoy very limited success and live far below their potentials is often because they are afraid of leaving the known for the unknown. The reason many companies cannot experiment and expand their product and service lines is because of the fear of failure. The reason many churches refuse to grow, with no visible presence in any other place after many years of starting, is fear.

Many people prefer to stay stuck to their comfort zones out of fear, forgetting that what they consider to be a place of comfort is actually a place of danger. The reason is simple. Complacency has no place in God's original plan for our lives. The day we stop being better is the day we stop being good.

My point here is that fear causes complacency and with complacency comes depreciation and retrogression. Alex and Brett Harris in their book, Do Hard Things, explain that complacency is a blight that saps energy, dulls attitudes, and causes a drain on the brain. They further described the two symptoms of complacency - satisfaction with things as they are, and rejection of things as they might be – adding that it is a state of mind where "good enough" becomes the watchword for today and the standard for tomorrow. "Like water, complacent people follow the easiest course - downhill. They draw false strength from looking back."

7. Fear attracts God's displeasure and other ills.
Well, this is inevitable for a number of reasons. First, fear is not in God's nature and no parent will be happy

to have children who are living below their potentials. Second, manifesting fear is a direct disobedience to God's repeated instruction to us in several passages of the Scripture not to fear. Third, our fear is a direct insult to His personality. It shows that we believe that the external forces or challenges are greater than His own majesty. Fourth, it shows that we do not believe that He cares enough for us to keep us from harm and misfortunes. Five, it shows that we believe that His numerous promises to protect us and supply all our needs can fail; that He can be unfaithful.

Our God is omnipotent, omnipresent and omniscient. And when we demonstrate fear in whatever circumstances, we are simply doubting and denying these infinite attributes of His. What usually follows is not often in our interest. The children of Israel can attest to this. When they got an evil report concerning the land that God had promised them, rather than look up to God who had given the promise, they gave in to fear and discouragement and started making negative confessions about their lives. And God ensured that their declarations came to fulfilment. "And the Lord spoke to Moses and Aaron, saying, "How long shall I bear with this evil congregation who complain against Me? I have heard the complaints which the children of Israel make against Me. Say to them, 'As I live,' says the Lord, 'just as you have spoken in My hearing, so I will

Why You Must Prevail Over Fear

do to you: The carcasses of you who have complained against Me shall fall in this wilderness, all of you who were numbered, according to your entire number, from twenty years old and above." (Numbers 14:26-29).

Job, too, testified that most of his misfortunes had risen from his fears. He said, "For the thing I greatly feared has come upon me, and what I dreaded has happened to me. I am not at ease, nor am I quiet; I have no rest, for trouble comes" (Job 3:25-26).

What all these revelations point to is that fear is a destructive fire that must be extinguished as soon as the enemy tries to kindle it in our lives. Without this, it may degenerate into a wildfire that has the potential to consume our peace, joy, progress and destiny. But I pray that this will not be your portion.

4

THE OTHER SIDE OF FEAR

"Everything you want is on the other side of fear."

—Jack Canfield

So far, we have been able to establish the truth that "fear is a darkroom where negatives develop." And I'm sure you are eager to discard every weight of fear from your life and fully become the person that God has created you to be. We will shortly be looking at how to dismantle the stronghold of fear, but before then, I'd like to give you a glimpse of what awaits you on the other side of fear. In addition to my experience which I shared in the first chapter, I will be relating the stories of some other people here to show you that loads of wonders and possibilities await you, once you can cast off the veil of fear from your life.

I want you to understand that the fear in your life is very much similar to the tares that the enemy sowed among the wheat in the parable told by Jesus in Matthew 13:24-30. Why do you think the enemy took the pains of sowing the tares, rather than killing the wheat altogether? Well, the intention was most likely to give the impression that the wheat was alive, while severely limiting its capacity to fully develop and produce in abundance.

This is exactly what fear is meant to do in your life; it is meant to hinder you from maximizing your potential and fulfilling your destiny. Affirming this, Joseph Campbell says, "The cave you fear to enter holds the treasure you seek." But I am sure you will prevail.

So, what awaits you when conquer your fears?

1. You will discover and fulfil your purpose in life.

George Washington Carver became one of the greatest scientists and inventors of the past century simply by refusing to give in to fear. He had been born of slave parents towards the end of the slavery period in the United States. Sadly, both his parents died shortly after his birth; so he and his elder brother were adopted into the household of their parents' masters, Mr. and Mrs. Carver.

Now, the challenge was that Carver had been born a very sickly child. In fact, he wrote in his autobiography in later years that much of his childhood was characterized by sickness. Things got worse when the family doctor once examined him and declared that he wouldn't live past the age of 21. Considering this and the fact that he was a very feeble child who couldn't do much of the field work that male children in general (slaves or not) were meant to do, he was limited to staying within the premises of the family's home.

Interestingly, however, instead of allowing his ill-health and the prediction of early death to dampen his spirits, Carver decided to take advantage of his situation to do something meaningful with his life. He learned to assist Mrs. Carver in doing domestic work and, in doing so, mastered the art of home-keeping. The valuable lessons he learnt within that period would prove so useful to him later on. But more importantly however was the fact that he spent his spare time in the house tending to the plants within the garden. He soon developed a powerful bond with plants and demonstrated such exceptional skills in gardening that people began to call him "the plant doctor". Even at that young age, people from all parts of the community were coming to him for advice on gardening.

When the time came for Carver to attend school and there was none he could attend in Missouri where he had grown up (being a black pupil) he quickly grabbed the opportunity to attend school in faraway Neosho

(Kansas). When the Carvers asked him how he would survive on his own, he told them he would find a place to work as a domestic help and attend school at the same time. Despite the fears expressed by his adoptive parents, Carver refused to be bothered. He went to Neosho and his optimism prevailed as he indeed found a kind family to lodge with.

As it had been with him from the beginning, Carver made the most of his time and never allowed the thought of impending "death" to weigh him down in any way. He excelled in his studies and, soon, it was time for him to attend high school. He left Neosho and moved to Fort Scott, depending on the money he had saved while working as a domestic help. For some reasons, when the Carvers heard that he had moved to Fort Scott, they were not happy. According to him, "When they heard from me, I was cooking for a wealthy family in Ft. Scott, Kansas, for my board, clothes, and school privileges. Of course, they were indignant and sent for me to come home at once to die, as the family doctor had told them I would never live to see 21 years of age."

You know what? Having consistently refused to be confined by fear, Carver would go on to live for much longer than the years predicted for him. In fact, he lived till old age. And not only that, he conquered bad health and lived a very productive life. But the most important fact is that it was while the fear of death and the limitations of ill-health were hovering over him that he found his purpose for life – botany and agriculture. That love that he had developed for plants in his childhood years guided his choice when it was time to attend university and settle for a career. And it was through this that he was able to impact the lives of many American farmers and citizens in ways that no one could have imagined that any black man could. His experiments with peanuts and other plants led to the invention of hundreds of products and founding of many industries for processing of agricultural products, especially the peanut. In fact, by the time of Carver's death, the peanut which was once a despised crop had become a $200 million industry and a chief product of Alabama through his efforts!

Carver lived a fulfilled life, made so much impact and won several recognitions. This was what the fear of death wanted to prevent him from having but he refused to be caged and successfully got the benefits awaiting him on the other side of fear. I pray that this will be your testimony too!

2. You will exceed expectations.

I don't know the kind of childhood experiences you had or the sort of comments that have been made about you that seem to be trying to make you feel that you can never do well in life; or that you cannot succeed in a chosen field. Tell you what? Those negative experiences and comments are only meant to build a wall of fear around you and prevent you from being the best you can be. If you can choose not to be grounded by this barricade, you will discover on the other side that neither the mistakes of your past nor the criticisms of the present can define your destiny if you don't allow them. As Susan Boyle said, "There are enough people in the world who are going to write you off. You don't need to do that to yourself."

I'm happy that Boyle herself spoke from experience when she said that. She proved to be a quintessential example of someone who refused to allow criticism define her worth or confine her to mediocre living. Born when her mother was 45 years old, Boyle was the youngest of four brothers and five sisters. She was raised thinking that she had been briefly deprived of oxygen during a difficult birth resulting in a learning disability. She endured much bullying in school throughout her younger years.

Fortunately for Boyle, she realized early enough that she had a passion and talent for signing and she spent much of her time developing this. After winning some local competitions, her mother felt it was time for her to broaden her reach and impact. But there was a problem, Boyle had always had issues with her body

The Other Side of Fear

image. Not with all the bullying she had received, she never considered herself attractive enough to enter any major singing contest. In fact, according to her former coach, she abandoned an audition for The X-Factor because she believed people were being chosen for their looks.

Somehow, through encouragement, she gradually decided to act against her fears. In August 2008, she applied for an audition for the third series of Britain's Got Talent and was accepted, after a preliminary audition in Glasgow. When Boyle first appeared on Britain's Got Talent at the city's Clyde Auditorium, she had two major fears to confront - her looks, which she wasn't so sure about; and her age which was nearing 50. And indeed, when she mounted the podium, most of the audience booed her for her looks. Then when she announced, in reply to a question, that her dream was to become one of the most famous musicians in history, many even booed her the more. She seemed like the worst joker ever.

But Boyle wasn't moved by such widespread skepticism. Even though, according to her, she was "absolutely gobsmacked" by such negative reactions from the audience, she went on to deliver a stunning performance that held everyone spellbound. Even the judge, Amanda Holden, was forced to remark that her performance was the "biggest wake-up call ever" for all the mockers.

Now, the most cheering part is that not only did Boyle excel at that competition but the album she released later that year, I Dreamed a Dream, became the UK's fastest-selling debut album of all time. In the US, the album sold 701,000 copies in its first week, the best opening week for a debut artist in over a decade. It topped the Billboard chart for six straight weeks. Indeed, in just one week, Boyle's debut album sold more than 2 million copies worldwide, becoming the fastest selling global female debut album.

When Boyle was later asked why she wasn't fazed by people's initial attitude when she went for her audition, she replied, "I know what they were thinking, but why should it matter as long as I can sing? It's not a beauty contest."

What if this amazing woman had allowed the fear of bullies and mockers to get the better part of her? Your guess is as good as mine that she might have forever been confined to the obscurity of her local community.

You will have the same wonderful story to tell, if you can choose to get to the other side of your fears!

3. You will achieve the impossible.

When Ben Carson decided to push aside all the fears that had existed both in his mind and throughout the medical world to attempt separating a set conjoined

The Other Side of Fear

twins in September 1987, he never would have imagined that he was going to be setting a new record that would astound the world. Before the revolutionary operation, which he led 70 other surgeons to perform, he had been worried about how Siamese twins could be successfully separated without the catastrophe that usually occurred in the wake of such an operation.

Of course, because a few previous attempts at separating conjoined twins had failed in the past, most surgeons avoided venturing into the territory altogether. As I already stated, Carson too had his fears, but instead of allowing the fear to cage him, he decided to address it. According to his own narration, he had an extensive discussion with a specialist friend of his, Dr. Bruce Reitz, on the issue. He got some valuable insights from him, but he needed more. So, he approached another friend of his, a cardiothoracic surgeon, who sometimes operated on the heart of infants.

With the ideas gathered from these friends and others, Carson embarked on a five-month intensive training program with his team, in preparation for the very challenging procedure. In a nutshell, when the day for the procedure finally came, after a twenty-two hour period of painstaking surgery, the twin boys who were joined at the back of the head and shared a portion of the same brain, were successfully separated. And guess what? Both survived – first time in history! They were named Benjamin and Patrick respectively, in honor of the leading surgeons in their successful separation.

Again, not only did Carson become globally famous for this achievement and similar others, but he also opened a new chapter in the history of the medical profession. And since that time many more conjoined twins have been successfully separated all over the world.

Essentially, what had seemed impossible since time immemorial became possible because some subdued their fears. I believe you are next in line to set a new world record. Say an "amen" to that – and take the necessary actions after that!You will surpass your own "best".

Timanthes of Sicyon was an ancient Greek painter of the 3rd century BC. Following the success he recorded with one of his works, he simply assumed that he had reached the peak of his ability. With the widespread attention and accolades generated by that work, he wouldn't dare attempt another for fear of doing something less successful. So, he simply contented himself with admiring the beautiful piece of work every day.

However, something drastic and very interesting happened. One morning, Timanthes rushed to where his beloved painting was, only to find it smeared and badly defaced. The young artist was horrified and livid.

The Other Side of Fear

He rushed to where his master was to report to him and the older man told him it was he who had done it. "I did it for your own good," said the master. "That painting was retarding your progress. Start again and see if you can do better."

Though devastated and dismayed, Timanthes reluctantly agreed to do as he was told. Guess what? He ended up creating a work that far exceeded the former in beauty and magnificence. In fact, to date, that painting, which is called "The Sacrifice of Iphigenia", remains the most celebrated and the most enduring of all his works. A copy of this work is one of the treasured collections kept in a section of the museum in Naples, Italy.

Timathes produced this evergreen masterpiece because he overcame the fear of failure. I tell you, reader, something greater than you've ever achieved awaits you on the other side of fear. Whatever successes you may have recorded so far, trust me, your best is yet to come!

4. You will become a trailblazer.

The dictionary defines trailblazer as "a person who makes, does, or discovers something new and makes it acceptable or popular; or a person who marks or prepares a trail through a forest or field for other people to follow." Whichever of these definitions you prefer, Elizabeth Blackwell's life perfectly fits the picture. She had been destined to be the first woman to graduate as a medical doctor in the United States and beyond. But there was a problem. She had a fear of blood. Anything that had to do with blood irritated her and she avoided it as much as possible.

With that fear, she was about taking a destiny detour by going into the teaching profession. But, then, something happened that jolted her back to the call of destiny. A very close friend of hers died because she was not properly treated by the male doctor who had attended to her. Of course, in those days, there were no licensed female doctors. So, women who had health issues, no matter how sensitive it was, had to contact the male doctors. And you can easily imagine how extremely difficult it must have been for some of those women to open up to the male doctors.

So it happened that when this friend of Blackwell's was to die, she commented that she believed she would have survived if she had been treated by a woman. She consequently urged Blackwell to venture into the medical profession. That seemed to be the wake-up call that the young Blackwell needed and she resolved to bury her fear of blood to go into medicine.

Unknown to Blackwell, however, a greater barrier awaited her. In fact, it was as she began to make efforts to understand the requirements for entering the medical field that she realized the truth behind the lack of female physicians. That truth was that women were generally considered unfit, physically and mentally, to be allowed to study towards becoming medical doctors. Consequently, every effort Blackwell made was met with opposition.

But you know what? The fighter in Blackwell would not let her give in to such barriers. In actual fact, those barriers further helped to strengthen her resolve to open the doors of the medical profession to women. After several efforts, she was eventually admitted into the Hobart and William Smith Colleges in Geneva, New York, to study medicine.

Yet, that again proved to be the beginning of another battle for Blackwell. Not only was she the only female in a class of over a hundred students but she had to endure both the teasing of her classmates and the enmity of other people around. And through it all, she succeeded and graduated as the best student.

Because Blackwell successfully prevailed over her fears, she became a pacesetter, who not only uprooted age-long misconceptions about women's intellectual ability but she has since then inspired multitudes of other women to enter and excelled in the medical profession.

You can do this and much more as you overcome your fears too. Let's go on to discuss how you can do this!

5

ROUSE THE CHAMPION IN YOU

"One of the greatest discoveries a man makes, one of his great surprises, is to find he can do what he was afraid he couldn't do."

— **Henry Ford**

The 1972 Munich Games took a rather interesting turn when Australian swimmer, Shane Gould, who was just 15 years old joined other swimmers who were much older and more experienced than she was. Just before the commencement of the contest, a journalist walked up to her and asked how she hoped she would fare among her formidable opponents. Surprisingly, instead of expressing fear, Shane's answer was, "I have a feeling there will be a new world record today."

And indeed, an unforgettable world record was set that

Conquering Your Fears

day. Not only did Shane win that particular race but went on to win five individual medals, three gold (all in world record times), one silver and one bronze medal. In fact, at that very young age, within two years, she had broken 11 world records in six different events.

If you had asked Gould after the race whether she hadn't felt fear despite her courageous comment, she would have told you that she felt it but had to brace herself for a win anyway. You see, that's exactly how champions are made – not in comfort zones but on the battleground. And I want to particularly remind you that within the DNA of every child of God is the spirit of boldness, love and a sound mind. This means that you are not meant to be a weakling or a mediocre. You are not meant to be a loser or an underachiever. You have been fashioned and destined to be the head and not the tail; to be above only and never be beneath.

So, then, if God has not given you the spirit of fear, it means that fear should not have dominion over you or regulate any aspect of your life. It means you can exercise power and authority over fear at any time, just as you would any other force that wants to hinder your progress, limit your achievements or hamper your impact.

Here are the ways you can exert this dominion and break the hold of fear over your life:

Confront Your Fear

A behavioral expert once said, "People tend to avoid the situations or things they fear. But this doesn't help them overcome fear — in fact, it can be the reverse. Avoiding something scary reinforces a fear and keeps it strong."

This is the absolute truth. What you don't confront will continue to affront you. And there's no way you can master what you do not take time to understand. Marie Curie said, "Nothing in life is to be feared, it is only to be understood. Now is the time to understand more so that we may fear less." So, to conquer your fear, you must take some time to come face to face with it, rather than running from it.

David frequently adopted this approach in dealing with his battles with depression (See Psalms 42:11 and 43:5 for instance). Rather than allow himself to be swung about by the pendulum of depression, he chose to confront the enemy by identifying the source. He spoke thus: "Why are you cast down, O my soul? And why are you disquieted within me?"

You may need to do the same thing with your fear and ask, why exactly am I afraid? Is my fear justified? Is it solving any problem? Am I making necessary progress and living my best life with this fear? If not, why am I still allowing it?

Conquering Your Fears

One of the ways you can confront your fears is to go for counselling or have a discussion with those who may be contributing to this fear, perhaps unknowingly. If you are in an office or school setting, it may also be necessary to have a chat with any of those in positions of authority that can be of help to you.

Sometimes, though, the best way to stop leaving in an atmosphere of perpetual fear may be to quit the atmosphere or relationship altogether. Here is a typical scenario, as shared by Shanee Moret, a healthcare marketing expert, on LinkedIn recently:

My friend got demoted at work and has to train her replacement. She feels humiliated. Not only has she been stripped of her title and issued a pay cut, but when she asked whether the demotion was related to work performance, her boss gave her a vague reply: "We're restructuring…" What she really feels is that she failed to play the office politics game effectively and is getting penalized for it. Now she goes to work every morning, fearing she will be fired the moment she is done training the new manager – to the point where it's causing her to live in a constant state of anxiety and stress. She called Courtney and me, in tears, to ask for advice on what to do next. We told her to update her resume, network and to plan her departure…

That's a strategy for addressing that particular situation.

And of course, different situations will require different approaches. But my point here is, whatever it is that constantly causes you fear, worry or anxiety must be addressed, not endured or ignored.

TAKE ACTION – DO IT AFRAID!

Rightly has Nelson Mandela said, "I learned that courage was not the absence of fear, but the triumph over it. The brave man is not he who does not feel afraid, but he who conquers that fear." That, my friend, is the secret of most people who have fulfilled their destinies, achieved the impossible, set new records and inspired others to greatness. They acted despite their fears.

What this means is that there is no mortal who is not tempted to be afraid, but what distinguishes the winners from the losers is their response to fear. While some submit to it, others bring it to submission by defying its dictates. So, whatever you are inspired to do, go ahead and do it. It is far better to try and fail than not to try at all and forever live with the regret of what might have been if you had tried. As Theodore Roosevelt once said, "Far better it is to dare mighty things, to win glorious triumphs, even though checkered by failure, than to take rank with those poor spirits who neither enjoy much nor suffer much, because they live in the gray twilight that knows neither victory nor defeat."

So, friend, do you want to sing but are afraid you won't sing well? Go ahead and sing anyway – most of the award-winning singers today had that fear too at the beginning. Do you want to write and you think your writing won't be interesting, go on and write anyway. Most of the best-sellers you read today were written "just for fun", until someone saw their worth. Stephen King, who is a veteran writer and bestselling author himself, gave this tip, "The scariest moment is always just before you start. After that, things can only get better."

Whatever it is you want to do, go on and do it, because that is the way to overcome fear. Dale Carnegie stated, "Inaction breeds doubt and fear. Action breeds confidence and courage. If you want to conquer fear, do not sit home and think about it. Go out and get busy." Ralph Waldo Emerson also said, "Do that which you fear to do and the fear will die."

This is a tactic I learned during my early years at school. Despite whatever daunting challenge I had in front of me, I would plunge through and do it anyway. And it often ended up being a sweet success story.

Be Loaded With God's Word

If there is an anchor to keep heart at rest amid the troubles and turbulences of life. It is a sound knowledge of God's word. When you realize that there is no accident in God's program and that nothing catches Him unawares concerning any of His children, then you would realize that you have nothing to be worried or fearful about. When you understand that you serve a God who can do all things and that you have a Father who has all it takes to meet your needs, then you cannot be worrying and fretting as ordinary people do.

Most importantly, as you realize that you serve a faithful God, who has given an assurance of solution and deliverance for every challenge or difficulty you may face, then you know that everything about your life is assured, insured and secure with Him. This understanding, which can only come through a deep familiarity with God's word, will keep you in peace in all situations. Moreover, since faith is the opposite of fear and faith can only be boosted through God's word, then it becomes paramount that you give attention to this word and meditate on it regularly.

I will devote the last chapter of this book to some precious promises that God has given to help you in all situations and keep you from being afraid. But let me quickly cite a few here. In Psalm 91, God promises that despite the prevalence of disasters, diseases and terrors around you, you and yours will enjoy uncommon protection and security. And in case you want to go for an exam or interview, meditate on the promise that you will be the head and not the tail (Deuteronomy 28:13) and also that the Lord will go before you and subdue every difficulty and opposition (Isaiah 45:2).

It is promises like these and others bordering on healing, deliverance, victory and provision that you must declare whenever Satan wants to bring fear to your heart or whenever you receive a negative report or comment from others. Let God be true and all men liars! (Romans 3:4).

Recall God's past faithfulnessHow many times have you been delivered from situations that you thought would consume you? How many times have you succeeded when you had thought you would fail? How many times have you received unexpected mercies, favors, miracles and provisions? How many times have you been spared from the evils and crises that were befalling others? How many times have succeeded where others have failed? How many times have you been discouraged and God delivered you?

I am sure there have been many such instances in your life. These are precious memories you need to recall whenever you are tempted to be afraid. Rest assured that the same God who helped and delivered you on those occasions is still very much able to deliver in every other challenge or difficulty that may come your way. David used this strategy in conquering fear and defeating Goliath. When Saul wanted to cause him to be afraid by saying, "You are not able to go against this Philistine to fight with him; for you are a youth, and he a man of war from his youth," he simply replied, "Your servant used to keep his father's sheep, and when a lion or a bear came and took a lamb out of the flock, I went out after it and struck it, and delivered the lamb from its mouth; and when it arose against me, I caught it by its beard, and struck and killed it. Your servant has killed both lion and bear; and this uncircumcised Philistine will be like one of them, seeing he has defied the armies of the living God." Moreover David said, "The Lord, who delivered me from the paw of the lion and from the paw of the bear, He will deliver me from the hand of this Philistine" (1 Samuel 17:33-37).

It is important that you too adopt this approach, so as not to be discouraged by what others think or how serious the challenge you have to face may seem. Recall your past successes, as well as God's unfailing mercies. As you focus on these, your faith and courage will receive a surge and the power of fear will be paralyzed in your life.

Cast Your Burden Before the Lord in Prayer

Of course, regardless of the number of motivational and psychological principles and strategies that we may talk about, none can deny that there will always be situations that confound the knowledge and understanding of man. There are situations that are so mysterious and baffling to human reasoning that we find ourselves inevitably tumbling into the void of fear. Fortunately, God who holds the secrets of the universe in His power has given us access to approach Him for answers to our dilemmas and solutions to our burdens. Hebrews 4:16 exhorts, "Let us therefore come boldly to the throne of grace, that we may obtain mercy and find grace to help in time of need." 1 Peter 5:7 too says, "Casting all your care upon Him, for He cares for you."

Even the smartest and the strongest of men will need this divine intervention every now and then because we are not meant to be able to successfully navigate the twists and turns of life independent of God, "for in Him we live and move and have our being" (Acts 17:28). Abraham Lincoln, who is regarded as one of the most successful American presidents, revealed the secret of his success thus, "I have been driven many times upon my knees by the overwhelming conviction that I had nowhere else to go. My own wisdom and that of all about me seemed insufficient for that day."

You can learn from this example and those of countless others who are daily drawing supernatural strength to help them combat and triumph over the daily challenges of life. No matter the enormousness of the battles or challenges you may face, you can avoid being overwhelmed by taking advantage of the provision of support and succor that the Almighty God has made for you. Philippians 4:6-7 encourages, "Be anxious for nothing, but in everything by prayer and supplication, with thanksgiving, let your requests be made known to God; and the peace of God, which surpasses all understanding, will guard your hearts and minds through Christ Jesus."

That, dear friend, is the key to lasting peace in life's raging storms!

6

FAILURE IS NOT THE END

"Success is not final, failure is not fatal: it is the courage to continue that counts."

—Winston Churchill

I have realized that one of the reasons many people stop pursuing their goals and allow fear to dominate their lives is because they have experienced failures in the past. After trying once and again without succeeding, they automatically assume that they are failures. They therefore give up trying altogether in order to avoid the awful feeling of failure all over again.

This experience is so common among the generality of humanity. Many times, when we work on accomplishing a goal or task, and we fail at it, we get discouraged. We then settle for less than what we could have achieved if we had merely taken another shot at it or given it a fresh perspective.

Let me say, however, that for people who diligently strive to conquer their fears, failure must be seen as just the fuel for greater determination and success in the future. So, if you have tried and failed in the past, you mustn't let that hinder your drive and passion.

Failure is Universal

Let me emphasize here that nobody is immune to failure. Everyone must experience it at one time or the other. In fact, all the successful people that you may know today have failed at one time or the other in the past. What made the difference in their lives is that they refused to be defined and confined by their failures. Rather, they learned from them and turned them to stepping-stones for their greatness. Affirming this, Henry Ford said, "The only real mistake is the one from which we learn nothing."

Failure is one of the most powerful avenues for us to learn. Indeed, this is practically the essence of failure – to make us know and master what we did not know previously and in so doing move closer and closer to our desired success. It is commonly said of Thomas Edison that, in his quest to invent the electric bulb, he made hundreds of unsuccessful attempts – to the point

Failure is Not the End

that people were coming to him to discourage him from continuing. However, what he used to encourage himself after each failed attempt was, "I have learned another way not to make the electric bulb."

And as he kept learning this way, he eventually arrived at his invention that has continued to bless the world. Someone who knew him closely once said of him: "If he hadn't failed, Thomas Edison might not have become America's most well-known and prolific innovator." In fact, at one time, Edison himself related an experience he had with one of his colleagues in the laboratory: "After we had conducted thousands of experiments on a certain project without solving the problem, one of my associates, after we had conducted the crowning experiment and it had proved a failure, expressed discouragement and disgust over our having failed to find out anything. I cheerily assured him that we had learned something. For we had learned for a certainty that the thing couldn't be done that way, and that we would have to try some other way."

Edison's case is similar to that of most of the other great men and women in history and in our contemporary times. And we have their very own words to confirm this. Iconic basketball player, Michael Jordan, told the secret of his success thus: "I've missed more than 9000 shots in my career. I've lost almost 300 games. Twenty-six times I've been trusted to take the game winning shot and missed. I've failed over and over and over again in my life. And that is why I succeed." George Bernard Shaw, one of the greatest literary writers of the 20th century said, "When I was young, I observed that nine out of ten things I did were failures. So I did ten times more work." Similarly, J.K. Rowling, the brain behind the popular Harry Potter series, said, "It is impossible to live without failing at something, unless you live so cautiously that you might as well not have lived at all, in which case you have failed by default."

Failure is Not Your Name

Regardless of what anyone may think or say concerning the efforts you are making now to reach your dream, it is up to you to ultimately see that you fulfil your aspiration. Don't let negative attitude or utterances distract you or dampen your spirits. You know yourself better than anyone else. You alone know where you are going and how much effort you are making to get there. In fact, it is very normal for people not to understand you. But you just must keep on pushing till your breakthrough comes.

You don't have to explain yourself to everyone now. Rather, concentrate your efforts on reaching your goal and when you do, your achievement will speak for itself. In 1902, for instance, the poetry editor of Atlantic Monthly returned a stack of poems to a writer with this

Failure is Not the End

note, "Our magazine has no room for your vigorous verse." That person was Robert Frost, who would later become one of the best known of all American poets. Interestingly, it wasn't only that magazine editor that initially rejected Frost's work. Frost actually spent the first forty years of his life in obscurity, as his efforts were repeatedly spurned by editors and publishers. Yet, as he continued to believe in himself and refused to be crushed, he went on to become a celebrated writer and four-time winner of the Pulitzer Prize in poetry.

In 1905, the University of Bern turned down a scientific dissertation from a budding researcher and described it as "irrelevant and fanciful." That researcher was Albert Einstein. And, of course, I'm sure you already know the details of how he went on to become one of the greatest scientists in history. Earlier, before then, in 1894, an English teacher had noted on a teenager's report card that he demonstrated "a conspicuous lack of success." In fact, his father had been so frustrated by his repeated lackluster performance at school that he once said to him, "If you cannot prevent yourself from leading the idle, useless, unprofitable life you have had during your school days…you will become a…social wastrel." That student was Sir Winston Churchill. He went on to become the Prime Minister of Britain!

Conquering Your Fears

REFUSE TO BE DISCOURAGED

Everyone is prone to discouragement and fear after trying and failing. However, as I have already emphasized in previous chapters, your attitude at such a critical time will determine whether the fear rules you or you will overcome it and go on to do grander things.

Laura Ingalls' initial attempts at publishing a book did not impress publishers but she refused to give up and continued to improve on her writing skills. She was 65 years old when her book "Little House in the Big Woods" was published and it became a mega success. She would go ahead to write another "Little House" series including the last one that came out at age 76.

There are many others like this courageous woman. And I share their experiences here to encourage you not to let failure poison your aspiration with fear.

OPRAH WINFREY

Oprah Winfrey is well known for her business prowess and phenomenal success. Along her journey to the top, she was constantly confronted with failure but chose to rise above it each time. She rose to become an incredibly successful business mogul, who was able to conquer her fears, walk through her failures, and turn them into a fortune.

Failure is Not the End

Oprah had a very troubled childhood. She grew up in severe poverty such that her mother, at some point, secretly put her up for adoption. Growing up as a child, Oprah went through many tough times, which negatively affected her self-esteem. She was eventually sent to live with her father, with whom she felt safe and secure.

Although he had little to no education, Oprah's father understood the value of education and encouraged her to read a book every week and write a book report, which she had to submit to him. He made her realize that she had to excel in school and make the most of her life. This was the beginning of a positive change in her life, and she began to excel academically. In no time, she became an honors student and earned a scholarship to further her education.

One of the first jobs Oprah held was that of a news reporter. Being a black female news reporter at that time was very rare. She was often picked on for making mistakes while she read the news. Unfortunately, she was eventually fired for being too emotional while reading reports, mispronouncing words, and being too 'dull and stiff' while casting news.

Oprah was devastated. However, she saw this as an excellent springboard to turn things around for good. Instead of spending time moaning the loss of her job, she took intentional steps to turn an otherwise awful situation into one of high resilience and subsequent fame and fortune.

The criticism about her being "too emotional" helped her to realize her ability to empathize and connect with other people's stories. It was shortly after this that she started her first talk show, which turned out to be the best thing that could have happened to her. In this new role and opportunity, she found her true calling and purpose in life.

In no time, the show became a hit, and everyone wanted a piece of the 'great pie' she had just baked. Today, Oprah has her own television network, known as the Oprah Winfrey Network (OWN). In a nutshell, through sheer courage and determination, Oprah found ways to use disappointments as stepping stones and ultimately build a very successful business empire and continues to inspire millions across the world.

Amy Adams

Amy Adams had just done a few episodes of the Dr. Vegas show, when she was sacked from CBS in 2005. According to the station directors, she wasn't good enough for the job. Interestingly, that was about the third consecutive television show from which she was being fired. Yet, she had always hoped to make it big

Failure is Not the End

on TV! At that point in her life, she was tempted to give in to discouragement. According to her, "I was really thinking I wasn't going to be doing this anymore. I thought the industry was telling me it wasn't going to happen."

Nevertheless, Amy refused to give in to her fears. Rather, she did something that would change her life forever. She seized the opportunity of the latest dismissal focus on a role she had gotten in an upcoming movie. She gave the role her all and that movie, Junebug, would eventually prove to be the catalyst for her long-awaited breakthrough. When the movie premiered at the 2005 Sundance Film Festival, Amy was given a special jury prize, which, in addition to the impressive reviews the movie had attracted, placed her in the spotlight. She would go on to land much bigger roles. Presently, she is among the highest-paid actresses in the world, aside from receiving several awards, including two Golden Globes.

Apparently, Amy succeeded because she didn't let her series of failures destroy her dream. And this is what I'm encouraging you to do, reader. That you have tried and failed doesn't mean you're destined for failure!

GAIL BORDEN

Gail Borden gave the world what we know as condensed milk. And even though he died a long time ago, his success story has continued to be a source of inspiration. In fact, on his gravestone, in Bronx, New York, is written this immortal saying of his that resonates with our discussion here: "I tried and failed. I tried again and again and succeeded."

Borden's story has become unforgettable because of his refusal to be discouraged in his various attempts at showing the world the possibilities of condensation. His first attempt was with an invention called "meat biscuit", a dehydrated beef product. Sadly, Borden did not achieve much success from this initiative. In fact, after investing most of his life's savings to produce the meat biscuit in commercial quantity, the company he established collapsed within a few years.

Undeterred, Borden decided to shift his focus to condensing milk, after watching some young children die of milk contamination.

Yet again, after investing his remaining life-savings to build a milk condensing plant, the plant failed within a short time. He got some money to start again, but that attempt also proved unsuccessful. Refusing to give up, Borden obtained the backing of a New York financier which enabled him to start again. This time around, his efforts paid off with the outbreak of the Civil War, and the resulting demand for longer lasting condensed milk by the Union army. Thus was Borden's success finally

Failure is Not the End

sealed as he recovered his former losses, enjoyed a thriving business and became a very wealthy man who supported several schools, churches and other charities.

ARIANNA HUFFINGTON

Arianna Huffington joined the race for the governorship recall election in California in 2003. However, as the October date set for the election drew near, she realized that she stood no chance of winning. Polls showed that she had only two percent support. In a nutshell, her campaign – with all she had invested in it - had been a flop. She had no other choice but to quit even before the election.

That was a hugely embarrassing experience for Arianna but rather than being discouraged or fearful, she chose to make the best of the opportunity that her seeming failure had just presented to her. Here's how she described her experience: "When I ran for governor of California in 2003, it was a failure—but I learned a tremendous amount about the power of the internet. I also learned a lot about myself, about communicating, being able to touch people's hearts and minds, and listening. All the things that were ingrained in me during the campaign definitely had an impact in forming the Huffington Post."

Cheeringly, Huffington Post which she co-founded two

years after her election defeat, has grown into such a big outfit that it has several international editions. It was recently ranked No. 1 on the 15 Most Popular Political Sites and also became the first commercially run United States digital media enterprise to win a Pulitzer Prize.

Arise and Shine

Of course, there are still many more inspiring stories I could have narrated here, but I believe that the ones we have explored so far should have convinced and galvanized your spirit to take your place among the stars. You are destined to be among the champions of destiny who will fulfill their purpose and leave their marks upon people's hearts and upon the earth as a whole. You have begun the quest already and I believe you will finish well and strong.

Let me remind you that fear is a thief! Its only goal is to keep you from moving forward and achieving your goals. As I said before, everyone, at some point in life, will inevitably be confronted and challenged by fear. Fear will oppose you, but instead of running away when it comes, face it. Always remember, every fear conquered opens the door to greater success.

So, from this moment, take the bold step to rise above your fears. Go on and do what you've always been afraid to do. Yes, you can!

7

DIVINE ASSURANCES IN FEARFUL TIMES

"God promises to keep His people, and He will keep His promises."

—Charles Spurgeon

As earlier mentioned, I have compiled here a list of some of the precious promises of God to keep your heart at peace when troubles seem to loom everywhere and the darts of fear, doubt and anxiety are flying all around you. Let these assurances from God boost your faith, as well as strengthen and fortify you against the wiles of the devil and the lies of the world - knowing full well that God will never default in any of His promises for His children.

Meditate on these promises and declare them as often as fears threaten to assail your mind.

Nahum 1:7. The Lord is good, a refuge in times of trouble. He cares for those who trust in him.

Psalm 84:11. For the Lord God is a sun and shield; the Lord bestows favor and honor; no good thing does he withhold from those whose walk is blameless.

Isaiah 40:31. But those who hope in the LORD will renew their strength. They will soar on wings like eagles; they will run and not grow weary, they will walk and not be faint.

Isaiah 43:2. When you pass through the waters, I will be with you; and when you pass through the rivers, they will not sweep over you. When you walk through the fire, you will not be burned; the flames will not set you ablaze.

Jeremiah 29:11. 'For I know the plans I have for you', declares the LORD, "plans to prosper you and not to harm you, plans to give you hope and a future.

Deuteronomy 31:8. The LORD himself goes before you and will be with you; he will never leave you nor forsake you. Do not be afraid; do not be discouraged.

Joshua 1:9. Have I not commanded you? Be strong and courageous. Do not be afraid; do not be discouraged, for the Lord your God will be with you wherever you go.

Divine Assurances in Fearful Times

Psalm 23:4. Even though I walk through the darkest valley, I will fear no evil, for you are with me; your rod and your staff, they comfort me.

Philippians 4:6-7. Do not be anxious about anything, but in every situation, by prayer and petition, with thanksgiving, present your requests to God. And the peace of God, which transcends all understanding, will guard your hearts and your minds in Christ Jesus.

Matthew 6:31-33. So do not worry, saying, 'What shall we eat?' or 'What shall we drink?' or 'What shall we wear?' For the pagans run after all these things, and your heavenly Father knows that you need them. But seek first his kingdom and his righteousness, and all these things will be given to you as well.

Proverbs 3:5-6. "Trust in the Lord with all your heart and lean not on your own understanding; in all your ways submit to him, and he will make your paths straight."

Matthew 7:9-11. Which of you, if your son asks for bread, will give him a stone? Or if he asks for a fish, will give him a snake? If you, then, though you are evil, know how to give good gifts to your children, how much more will your Father in heaven give good gifts to those who ask him!

2 Corinthians 9:8 And God is able to bless you abundantly, so that in all things at all times, having all that you need, you will abound in every good work.

Psalm 34:10. The lions may grow weak and hungry, but those who seek the Lord lack no good thing.

Romans 8:32. He who did not spare his own Son, but gave him up for us all—how will he not also, along with him, graciously give us all things?

Mark 11:24. Therefore I tell you, whatever you ask for in prayer, believe that you have received it, and it will be yours.

Psalm 37:4. Take delight in the Lord, and he will give you the desires of your heart.

John 14:13. And I will do whatever you ask in my name, so that the Father may be glorified in the Son. You may ask me for anything in my name, and I will do it.

NOTES

NOTES

NOTES

NOTES

NOTES

www.ingramcontent.com/pod-product-compliance
Lightning Source LLC
LaVergne TN
LVHW051847080426
835512LV00018B/3123